As-salamu alaikum! Peace be upo[illegible]

We are excited and hopeful abou[illegible] society. The purpose of this booklet is to help you remain, and succeed in free society. We believe you will be among the successful. It will take faith, patience and work. Our prayers are with you.

About this Booklet

This booklet was developed for Muslim men and women who are being released from prison. However, it has a lot of information and advice that can be helpful for reentry, regardless of faith.

About Tayba Foundation

At Tayba Foundation, we believe that all people contain a wellspring of goodness within them, and we believe in the power of human potential.

Even when individuals encounter dramatic setbacks in life, lasting change is possible.

Tayba Foundation is a non-profit organization dedicated to serving individuals and families impacted by incarceration. We believe in the power of human change through holistic education, guidance, and support.

TAYBA FOUNDATION

Freedom Through Education

Tayba instructors are here to provide further guidance and brotherly support.
They can be contacted by phone:

803-415-4551 **(510)-491-7859** **(510)-491-6165** **(510)-641-8881**

by email: instructors@taybafoundation.org or by mail:

Tayba Foundation
PO BOX 1154 Portsmouth
NH 03802

Written by *Sheima Sumer*
Graphic design by *Sana Siddiqui*
Edited by *Nusayba Elqabbany* and *Umm Ahmed*

Table of Contents

01 Before Release:

"If you fail to plan, you plan to fail."

The Importance of Planning

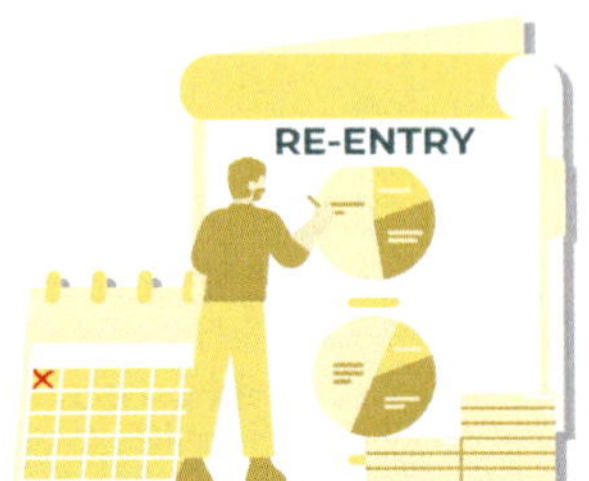

Planning is part of Islam. You should prepare for reentry about **3-6 months** before your release date.

Consider the following hadith of Mu'adh Ibn Jabal (Allah be pleased with him):

> The Prophet (ﷺ) sent Mu'adh to Yemen to teach people about Islam.
>
> The Prophet ﷺ asked Mu'adh before he left:
> *"Oh Mu'adh! How will you judge between the people if you are asked to?"*
> Mu'adh responded, *"With the book of Allah."*
> *"What if you don't find what you're looking for in the book of Allah?" the Prophet asked.*
> *"Then with the Sunnah of the Messenger of Allah,"* he replied.
> *"What if you don't find what you're looking for in the Sunnah?"* questioned the Prophet.
> *"Then I will make a decision based on my judgment,"* he answered.
>
> **(Tirmidhi)**

This hadith shows that the Prophet ﷺ would not allow Mu'adh (RA) to go on his mission without a plan. He ﷺ asked Muadh (RA) questions to make sure he had a plan.

In this preparation phase you will need to do the following:

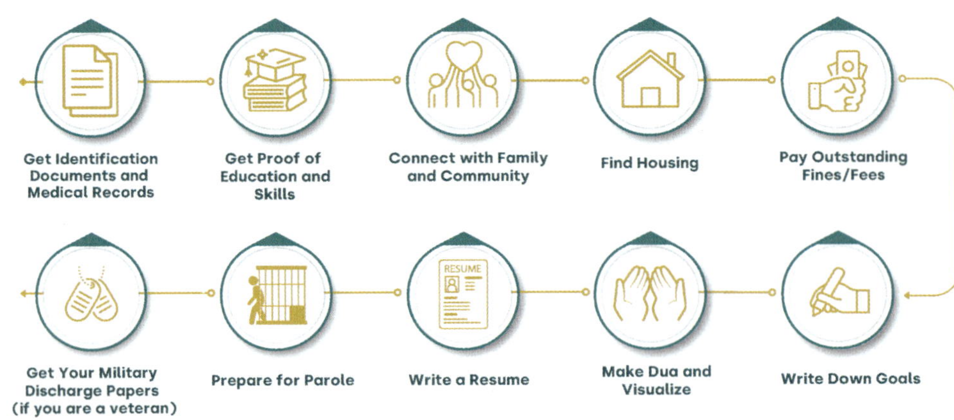

GET IDENTIFICATION DOCUMENTS AND MEDICAL RECORDS

You need your **social security card, birth certificate and ID.** It's harder to get these once you're out of prison. Your case manager can help you. It will take time and multiple steps to get these documents. Your family may have to contact government agencies in your county of birth. Keep your social security card in a safe place.

You should also obtain your medical records. You will need them to get medical treatment. Health Services should help you to get your medical records.

GET PROOF OF EDUCATION AND SKILLS

You need to get proof of your **GED/high school diploma and classes/activities** you did in prison. You'll need these when you apply for jobs. Please contact your Tayba instructor to provide a transcript of courses you've taken with us.

Tayba strongly recommends that you take classes to help with reentry, even if they're not required for parole. One example is **WRAP**, (Wellness Recovery Action Plan). You may have already taken this course with Tayba Foundation. If that was a long time ago, you may want to review it now.

CONNECT WITH FAMILY AND COMMUNITY

Family and community are a huge source of support when reentering society. Be honest with them about what you need–whether it's housing, money, or just support and love–but do not solely rely on them, overburden them or guilt-trip them into helping financially. Patiently listen to their needs, concerns and expectations. Reuniting will be easier when you talk ahead of time. Get to know the masjids (mosques) in your city/area.

HOUSING

Statistics show that ex-offenders without housing are at the highest risk of returning to prison. Family and friends are the top sources of stable housing. Make sure that your family is aware of any requirements of your probation while living with them.

If you are unable to live with family or friends, you may live in a halfway house or transitional housing. One helpful website is transitionalhousing.org

OUTSTANDING FEES/FINES/ WARRANTS

Ask your case manager if you have any outstanding fines, fees, debts, or warrants. These can lead to problems with getting a job, housing, and even arrest. Outstanding child support payments can prevent you from getting a driver's license.

WRITE DOWN GOALS

Writing down your goals helps you achieve them faster. Take time to reflect on your personal goals. Then go through each one and write down how you can achieve it. For example, to find a job you need to write a resume, search for jobs and then apply for jobs. Put your goal list in a place where you can see it every day.

DUA

Never underestimate dua: calling on Allah (ﷻ) and asking Him for help. A former Tayba student, Amin Rafiq, is living proof of the power of dua.

Here is Amin's story, as told by Shaykh Rami:

"Amin had three life sentences given to him when he was a juvenile, just 17, for a non-violent drug offense, but he never gave up hope. What gave him that hope was his belief in the Power of Allah to change anything, and the ability of a Muslim to connect to that Power through dua. Amin said he was consistent and sincere in his dua. One year I went to 'umrah and I made dua for Amin while at the Ka'bah and in front of the Messenger of Allah (peace be upon him). I really wanted him to be released. Years later, Amin told me that when I told him about that dua, he *knew* he would be released. When I asked why he felt that, he said, "Because you lifted my name up in dua to Allah at His house." A few years after that 'umrah, Amin was released. It was truly a miracle, given that he had been handed three life sentences."

WRITE A RESUME

A resume is a summary of your skills, work experiences, and strengths. You can handwrite your resume while in prison and then type it after your release. The employment section of this booklet has more details on writing a resume and finding a job.

PREPARE FOR PAROLE

When you are released from prison, you will generally be on parole or probation, which means you will be supervised by your state's Department of Corrections for a period of time. You will have to follow rules for your parole, which can be frustrating. With patience and determination to improve your life, you will get through it. Before your release you should:

- Learn about the **requirements** of your parole
- Find a place to live
- Tell the people you'll be living with how your parole may affect them
- Make sure you have your parole officer's name and number because you may need to call him/her within **24 hours of release**
- Complete all paperwork

FOR MILITARY VETERANS

If you are a veteran, you need to get your military discharge papers. Your case manager can help. Military veterans receive many government benefits. It is permissible (halal) to accept money from a non-Muslim government as long as you don't lie for benefits or need to do something forbidden.

As a veteran you receive special benefits related to healthcare, basic needs (food and housing), education, employment and legal services. For more information, call **1-800-393-0865** (general benefits), **1-877-424-3838** (housing benefits) or visit the website **benefits.va.gov** after release.

02 The First 72 Hours:

Connect to Resources

72 HOURS

The first 72 hours are critical to your success. Call your parole officer within the first 24 hours. Take responsibility for developing connections.

Make every effort to stay away from relationships that could lead you to sin or bad habits. Find a mentor or someone you trust. If you don't have anyone suitable for this, you can ask your Tayba instructor to help hold you accountable.

This section will talk about the following steps you need to take in this critical time:

Connect with the Muslim Community

Get a Smart Phone

Get your Photo ID

Confirm Selective Service Status if you're under 26

Get Health Insurance

Seek Employment

Connect with Tayba instructors and coaches

Tayba's instructors can be reached by email: instructors@taybafoundation.org or contacted by phone: (510)-491-7859 (510)-491-6165 (510)-641-8881

Getting a Phone

You need a phone to communicate with family, friends, parole officers and employers. You can get a basic cell phone which works for calls and messaging. A smartphone (which is more expensive) is a cell phone with internet capability.

Phone options will be covered in Part 4: "Technology Literacy". You can also use landline phones, which are connected to one place.

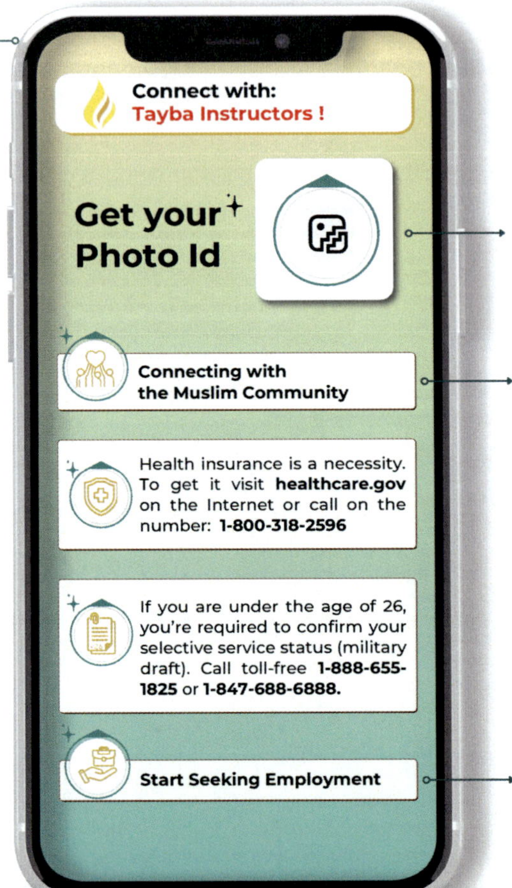

You will need to get your photo ID at a local **DMV (Department of Motor Vehicles)**. Use the internet to find your local DMV (search "DMV near me") and search what documents to bring. Usually you need to bring your birth certificate and/or social security card.

Connecting with your Muslim community will be an important factor in your success. Visit the masjid as much as possible. You should get a list of masjids in your city before your release.

Finding a job is extremely important for staying out of prison. **Goodwill.org** is one organization that helps ex-offenders find jobs. More websites are listed in the "Employment" section of this booklet. You can talk to people in your community and see if they have any ideas for opportunities. For more details on finding and keeping a job, see Part 5: "Employment"

Other Resources

For more resources you can call **211** or visit **211.org**. This is a free confidential service that helps people find local resources 24/7 (food, housing, health-care, transportation, etc.)

Other organizations that provide help are the National Reentry Resource Center, United Way, and the Salvation Army. Also:

https://georeentryconnect.com/resource-map/ - for all sorts of emergency needs based on location
https://www.transitionalhousing.org/ - for emergency housing
www.assurancewireless.com - (888) 321-5880 free wireless government phone service

03 Staying Out of Prison:

Why do 75% of ex-offenders return to prison within 5 years?

Recidivism

is defined as "the re-arrest, reconviction, or re-incarceration of an ex-offender". Data indicates that **68%** of released prisoners are rearrested within 3 years of release. Over **75%** are back in prison within 5 years of release and **83%** within 9 years*.

*US. Bureau of Justice Statistics

8 Reasons for Recidivism

Same Reason as the First Time

The reasons for reoffending are often the same as the first time. Reflect on what caused you to offend the first time and don't repeat the cycle.

Bad Social Group

Many ex-offenders return to prison because they reconnect with the same friends/partner that got them in trouble in the first place. You need to leave the harmful people in your life. The Prophet ﷺ said: "A person is on the religion of his companions. Therefore let everyone of you carefully consider the company he keeps." (Sahih Tirmidhi)

No Employment

Being unemployed is a major cause of recidivism. Not being able to provide for yourself can lead to a lower standard of living than in prison. Getting a job is necessary.

No Housing

Being homeless greatly increases the likelihood of returning to prison, considering the crimes one would commit for survival.

Substance Abuse

Using drugs/toxic substances is a top reason why people return to prison.

Lack of Support and Feeling Overwhelmed

Adjusting back to society is not easy. You are moving from a structured environment to one where you need to figure everything out. If you don't have enough support from family, friends and community, this can lead to crime.

Parole Violations/Missing Appointments

Unfortunately this is a very common cause of ex-offenders recidivating. Violating your parole could land you back in prison.

Self-Sabotage

This may be hard to accept, but some people subconsciously want to return to prison because it is what they are used to. The mind doesn't like change and prefers the familiar. In such cases, the former-prisoners self-sabotage and do things to return to prison.

Advice to reduce your chance of going back to prison

1. Keep Up Your 5 Daily Prayers (Salah) and the Friday (Jumuah) Prayer

"Truly the prescribed prayer keeps (one) away from indecency and wrongdoing" (Quran 29:45). Regularly performing prayer protects you from doing sinful acts and keeps you connected with Allah.

For men, it's important to attend the Friday prayer at your masjid because missing it can make one become heedless of Allah. The Prophet ﷺ said: *"People need to stop neglecting the Friday prayers, lest Allah place a seal over their hearts and then they become heedless." (Sahih Muslim)*

2. Make Housing a Priority

Statistics show that ex-offenders without housing are at the highest risk for recidivism. Those who are homeless can call 1-800-569-4287 (US Department of Housing and Urban Development) or search "homeless services near me" on the internet.

3. Distance yourself from harmful people

Being around harmful, toxic people leads many people back to prison. The Prophet ﷺ said, *"The likeness of good company and that of bad company is that of the owner of musk and of the one blowing the bellows. The owner of musk would either offer you some free of charge, or you would buy it from him, or you smell its pleasant fragrance; and as for the one who blows the bellows (i.e., the blacksmith), he either burns your clothes or you smell a repugnant smell."* (Bukhari and Muslim)

4. Write Down All Parole Officer Appointments/Duties

Missing PO appointments and violating parole leads many people back to jail. Make sure to communicate with you PO if you are having any issues meeting your appointments. If you follow the rules, your parole period will end with ease.

5. Stay Busy with Positive Activities/Hobbies

Find groups to join that will you busy and healthy. Examples include sports groups, classes, programs at your local library or community center.

6. Get Help if you suffer from a Substance Abuse Problem

Substance abuse is a leading cause of returning to prison. You can call 1-800-662-HELP (4357) or search "substance abuse treatment near me" on the Internet.

7. Create a Support System

Stay in contact with people/organizations who can help and support you. Don't let your ego (nafs) keep you from asking for help when you need it.

Start creating a support system before you leave prison. People often feel lonely after prison and join toxic social groups because they don't have other options. Pray to Allah to give you good company.

7. Plan for Release Before Your Release Date

Connecting with support before release will make your life much easier. Make a plan on how you will achieve your goals. Write it down. See "Part 1: Before Release."

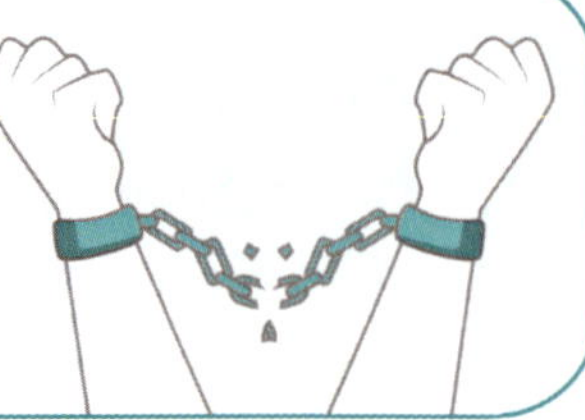

9. Be Aware of Self-Sabotage

Self-sabotage is when we get in the way of our own success. It can be conscious or subconscious. We self-sabotage when we are afraid of change. Change is new, unfamiliar, and scary. Be aware that the mind (ego) prefers the familiar over the unfamiliar, which is why many ex-offenders do things to return to prison. Be open to stepping into the unfamiliar world of a successful life.

04 Technology Skills:

An Unexpected Challenge

Technology literacy may be the most important skill for successful reentry. If you can use technology (computers, smartphones, etc.), then you can use it to learn many other skills.

Learning new technologies is one of the most unexpected challenges of reentry. You need computers and phones to communicate, apply for jobs, pay bills, and more.

The easiest way to learn how to use a smartphone, computer and other technologies is to ask someone to teach you. Remember to be patient with yourself as it may take time to pick up the basics.

Basic Terms:

SEARCHING ON THE INTERNET

- Google
- wikihow.com
- Youtube
- Use key words while searching

THE INTERNET

- Wi-Fi (wireless internet connection)
- Security & Passwords
- Email
- Smartphone/Computer

OTHER USEFUL FEATURES

- Google Drive
- Google Docs/Maps
- WhatsApp
- Telegram/Zoom
- Facebook/Messenger

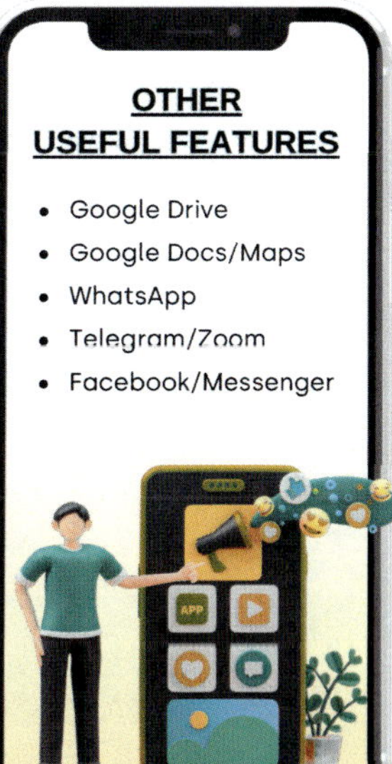

THE INTERNET

The internet connects computers and phones all over the world. If you don't have your own computer or smartphone, you can go on the internet at most libraries. You may need a photo ID. "Online" means "on the internet." "Wi-fi" refers to a wireless internet connection.

SEARCHING ON THE INTERNET

- You can search for any information on the internet by typing a word, phrase or question into the search bar and pressing "search" or "enter" (for example: "what is..." or "how to...). Popular search websites include Google.com. Once you see results, click on the result you want to read.
- You can also search for services in your area by adding "near me." For example, you can search "masjids near me" or "halal restaurants near me" and you will see local information.
- The results can seem overwhelming. Often the first results are paid advertisements and may not be what you're looking for. Remember that you can always ask people in your community for help.
- A helpful website for "how-to" questions is wikihow.com. It clearly answers almost any how-to question (e.g. "how to find a job").
- YouTube.com is a website with billions of videos. You can search on YouTube for information too, but your search results will be videos rather than websites.

E-MAIL (Electronic Mail)

An email address is needed for online communication. You can create an email address for free with: https://mail.google.com

1. ACCOUNT SET UP:

- **STEP ONE:**
- Go to the above website and click on "Create Account
- Fill out the required information, then choose your email address. Keep it simple and professional: first name and last name or a combination of initials/numbers (e.g. johndoe@gmail.com). In order to protect yourself from identity theft, do not use your birthday year or month.

- **STEP TWO:**

- If an email address is already taken, you will see an error and you will need to choose a different email address. Click "Next" to continue. Click "agree" to the conditions and terms. You will need to choose an email password.

- **STEP THREE:**

- Save your password somewhere private and safe because many people forget their passwords.

- Using email is straightforward and just needs practice. You can always ask a family member, friend or librarian for assistance.

COMPOSE AN EMAIL

STEP ONE:

- After logging into your account, you will see your "Inbox" which contains your received emails. Click "Compose" to write emails.

STEP TWO:

- Enter your recipient's email address in the "To" textbox. Enter the subject of your email in the "Subject" textbox and write the main message in the large textbox.

STEP THREE:

- You can attach files (such as a resume) to your email by clicking the paperclip symbol and then selecting files from your computer.
- You can reply to emails by opening the email and clicking the arrow at the top right that is pointing backwards (if you hover your mouse over the arrow, it says "Reply"). Remember that if the email is a group email, you can choose "Reply All" to reply to the whole group.

Sometimes emails will go to the "Spam" or "Junk" folder, so be sure to check there if you are expecting an email but don't see it in your Inbox. There is more to learn about email, which is why we recommend that you practice and search on the internet/YouTube "how to use email".

APPS (Application)

An App is a software program that's designed for a specific use. There are all kinds of apps that you can download to smartphones and computers. Common apps include Whatsapp, Telegram, Zoom, Google Maps, PayPal, Gmail, Muslim Pro, YouTube and more. To download apps on a smartphone go to the "App Store/ Play Store".

- You can also search the types of apps you want, such as "Quran Apps." Most apps can be downloaded for free but some have a small cost.

- Money and banking apps such as Zelle, PayPal, and Venmo help you to transfer money easily. Communication apps such as Whatsapp and Telegram allow you to send messages and call people for free using the Internet. Your family members can show you how to use these apps. You can download Gmail (and other email apps) to your smartphone as well.

GOOGLE DRIVE, GOOGLE DOCS & GOOGLE MAPS

- Google Drive is an app where you can save your files and documents on the internet. It's easy to share your files with others using Google Drive/Google Docs.

- Google Maps is an extremely helpful app that tells you directions to almost any place on Earth. Google Maps works with different modes of transportation: car, public transportation, walking, and biking. For more information on using these apps, ask family/friends or visit wikihow.com and type in "how to use (name of app)".

WHATSAPP, GOOGLE MEET, FACEBOOK, MESSENGER, FACETIME & TELEGRAM

- Whatsapp, Zoom, Google Meet, Facebook Messenger, Facetime and Telegram are apps that allow you to talk to one or more people online for free. You download these apps to your smartphone or computer. To download apps to a smartphone, you go to the "App Store/PlayStore" on your phone and search for the app you want to download.

- For Zoom and Google Meet, you share an internet link with people and you talk by clicking on the link. For WhatsApp, Messenger, Facetime, and Telegram you click on a "contact" in your contact list to call.

- If all of this technology is new to you, don't worry, you will get the hang of it in time.

05 Employment:

Find a Job, Keep a Job

Finding a job is one of the most important ways to protect yourself from returning to prison. Earning a living is a highly rewarded deed in Islam. Someone once asked the Prophet ﷺ, *"What are the best earnings?"* The Prophet ﷺ answered, *"An honest sale or a man's work with his hands."* (Musnad Ahmad)

Many employers are willing to give you a chance. Many ex-offenders have found good jobs. Be prepared, persistent, and positive and you will find a rewarding job insha'Allah.

Your Application Package

Put together an application package with your resume and cover letter, and a list of references and/or letters of recommendation.

A resume lists your past work experiences, skills, education and interests. Also include any certifications or formal training you completed in prison. A resume should describe what you did exactly for each job and what skills you learned. Resume examples can be found online. Just search "resume example for (type of job)". Microsoft Word and Google Docs have resume templates (a form you can type on that already looks like a resume). Your resume should include:

Resume

Name, & contact information

Education (attended schools, degrees, certificates)

Work Experiences (paid & volunteer work; location & tenure of the job)

Other professional skills (certifications, technical skills, languages you can speak, driver's license)

- skills that match what the job requires: Try to show you have what the job is looking for. E.g., if they want customer service skills, explain how you worked with customers in the past. For in-prison jobs you had, your employer can be the state where you were incarcerated.
- a cover letter: A cover letter is a one-page letter from you to the potential employer. It explains why you want the job and why you're the best person for the job. Cover letter examples can be found online.
- references: References are people who can discuss your experience, character traits and skills. You should have at least 2 references and provide their names, email addresses and phone numbers.

Good potential references are:

• Former/Current Employers • Teachers • Social Workers • Religious Leaders

Once you've created your application package, ask an experienced person to look through it and give you feedback.

Applying for Jobs (Tips)

Look for jobs that are a good fit for your skills and interests. You can still apply for jobs even if you don't meet every requirement.

- Talk to your counselor or parole officer about jobs that may not be suitable based on your previous offense. Many applications don't ask about felonies, but if they do, be honest and check "yes."
- Then write on the side: "will discuss at the interview."

- Today, most job applications are done online. Sometimes you can apply in person, which helps the employer connect with you and you may get the job faster.
- It's best to take entry level positions and then upgrade to a better job later. Don't feel discouraged if it takes time to find a job. Be patient and don't give up. *"Truly Allah loves the patient."* (Quran 3:146)

Helpful Websites to Find a Job

Careeronestop.org is a website of the Department of Labor. Not only can you search for jobs, but you can also find resume guides, interview tips and trainings. The phone number is 1-877-872-5627.

The American Job Centers system is also run by the Dept. of Labor. Job centers help you to find a job. You can search online "job centers near me" or find a center by calling the free helplines at 1-877-US-2JOBS or 1-877-889-5267.

in

You can also create a "LinkedIn" account. LinkedIn.com is a website that connects people in the working world. Many companies use LinkedIn to find employees. Just search for LinkedIn.com and and enter your name, email and password. Click "Join Now." Enter the other information that you are asked for. LinkedIn will send you an email which you need to open and click on a link to confirm your LinkedIn account. For more information, search "how to create a LinkedIn account".

Other helpful websites are:

- jobsforfelonshub.com
- jailstojobs.org
- jobsthathirefelons.org
- ziprecruiter.com
- indeed.com

Offline Ways to Find a Job

Some offline ways to find jobs are to:

- Newspapers' classified ads
- "Help Wanted" signs around the city

The Interview

Most applications don't lead to interviews. Be patient and keep applying. The more applications you put in, the higher your chance of getting an interview.

Prepare a list of your strengths and work experiences and be ready to talk about them. Be ready to answer questions such as: *What skills can you offer an employer? What are you good at?* What type of work do you enjoy? Practice the interview with someone.

AT THE INTERVIEW:

OFFLINE	ONLINE
• Be clean and well-dressed • Arrive 10-15 minutes early • Bring your resume, reference, contact information, social security card, pen and a notebook	• Test your Internet Connection • Test your video/audio • Pick a quiet place • Look presentable • Be punctual

If you have tattoos you would like to cover, you can look for a concealer (particularly useful for the face and neck), sleeves, or tape that covers exposed skin. Concealer resembles a thick, skin-toned lotion. Many stores sell this in the cosmetics section.

- Concealer is a barrier on the skin when making *wudu*. Ensure to remove it before doing your *wudu* and then reapply afterwards.

DURING THE INTERVIEW :

- Make eye contact
- Have good posture
- Be natural and smile
- Be polite and avoid slang talk
- Don't bring friends/family

- Keep it positive. Say: *"I thought a lot about where my life was going and I decided to make some changes."* Talk about your current activities and future career goals. Talk about your education, job training, community work and other activities.

- Encourage the employer to hire you. Say: *"I am a good worker. I want to work. I just need an opportunity to prove my skills."*

If you are asked about your criminal record, be honest. For example, you may say: *"At that time I was making some bad choices and I was convicted of..."* Answer any concerns the interviewer may have.

Redirect the interview back to your skills and what you bring to the job. Say: *"I can see why that might concern you. But that was several years ago. Today I am a hard worker and quick learner."* If your conviction is not related to the job you're applying for, say: *"Yes, I was convicted of a felony. But it was not job-related."*

Keeping Your Job and Moving up the Ladder

Take an entry-level position if it becomes available, even if it's not what you want long-term. Take advantage of the opportunities that come your way to get closer to your goal. Don't let your ego (nafs) get in the way of a good, halal opportunity.

In order to move to the next level:

- Be punctual
- Stand out
- Don't complain without a good reason
- Step away from negative talk

Remember to update your resume when you gain new work experiences and skills. As you gain more experience, you can apply to better jobs.

Education

Education expands your career options. Make sure you get your GED if you don't have a high school diploma. One website for this is: www.Finishyourdiploma.org. You can also search "GED classes near me" on google or call 1-800-626-9433. Once you have your GED or high school diploma, you may consider taking college classes at a community college.

06 Family & Community Reunification:

Connecting with Patience

Adjusting to Family Life

It will take time to get used to life back at home. Be patient with yourself, your family, and friends. Take small steps. Trust takes time to rebuild.

Your family will have changed over time. It will take time to get to know each other again especially if you were incarcerated for a long time. You may struggle to feel like you belong. Show your family that you care about their needs, are interested in what they are doing, and you want to spend time with them.

Your relationship with loved ones may go through different stages. Things might start out great (the "honeymoon" stage) but then get harder as you spend more time together.

Four common relationship stages during reentry:

1. Honeymoon:

You and your loved ones are excited to be back together. Everyone's at their best, but anxiety is beneath the surface.

2. Uncertainty:

Uncertainty about the relationship creeps in. You start to question each other's motives. Are you going to stick around? Do you still want to be together?

3. Sharing:

You will test each other to see if it's ok to share feelings and be yourself. Can you trust each other?

4. Belonging:

You may struggle to get involved in family routines. What roles will you play? How can you be part of family life again?

SELF-DISCLOSURE

Many ex-offenders survive prison by being "closed off" and isolated. But being closed off with family can harm your relationships. Self-disclosure is sharing truthful information about yourself. Self disclosure is important in relationships. Sharing honestly about yourself has the following benefits:

- Builds trust
- Provides emotional release
- Encourages your loved ones to share honestly with you

Here are some ways to open up to loved ones:

START WITH SMALL TALK
Talk about what they do for fun, how their day is going, what their plans are, etc.

SPEND TIME TOGETHER
Such as taking long walks and talking about your feelings, fears and goals.

LEARN TO TEXT
Send short, friendly messages about your day to family and friends. Ask how they are doing. Build rapport.

AVOID CRITICIZING
Focus on being a good listener, positive and supportive.

Be honest if you are asked about your incarceration. You don't need to act tough. Let them know that prison is no way to spend your life. Avoid talking about life in prison as your only conversation topic—make "small talk" about daily events instead.

If you are a parent, you may feel both excited and nervous about reuniting with your kids. You may feel guilt. You may want more time to adjust to society before getting your kids back. It's normal to have mixed feelings about seeing your children. There's no right way to feel.

- Children may not understand everything that has happened. You can ask them if they have any questions. Be patient as they adjust to having you back.
- If you are separated from your children, you may want to reunite with them right away. But don't rush things.
- First you need a stable job and housing. Getting your kids back too soon can sometimes cause more harm than good.

Challenges of Family Reunification

You may feel a range of difficult emotions when reuniting with loved ones: fear, sadness, grief, guilt and anger.

MAIN GOAL

Your main goal is to stay out of prison. No decision that might send you back to prison is good for your family. Your family is not supporting you if they expect you to do things that could land you back in prison. Sometimes your family's expectations are about what they believe is best for them and not you.

Family may blame you for causing harm to them with your past. The first step is to forgive yourself. Accept and make peace with your past mistakes and resolve to "make things right." Some relationships may never totally heal. Accept that your loved ones may not want the same relationship you once had.

- **ANOTHER CHALLENGE :**

Your family may not respect your religion. Again, it's best not to argue but to show Islam through your good character. The Prophet ﷺ advised people to be kind to family members that hate Islam, but to not allow those members to keep them from practicing Islam.

Do your very best to avoid toxic family and friends. It's better to be alone than to be with people who could lead you down the wrong path.

Muslim Community

It's necessary to connect with your Muslim community to protect your faith. Attend prayers and programs as much as possible. Many masjids have classes, and may offer support groups.

It's possible that you may be turned off by some Muslims and may even feel unwelcome. Be patient. It takes time to make friends and find like-minded people. If you're able, visit different masjids to see where you feel most comfortable. Remember your goal–to please Allah–and you will be less disappointed by people.

Connecting to the Larger Community

Getting involved in your community and making new friends will help you to heal from the trauma of prison life, insha'Allah. Here are some ways to get involved:

PUBLIC PARK

Spending time in nature increases wellbeing. Many parks offer sports and fitness programs.

REENTRY PROGRAMS

If there is a reentry program in your area, consider volunteering your time there.

LIBRARY

Public libraries have events, classes, & book clubs. They may also have a space where people post information about group meetings and job openings.

Marriage

Marriage is important in Islam. The Prophet ﷺ stated that marriage is "half of religion" (fear or consciousness of Allah being the second half). It's crucial to only participate in permissible (halal) relationships. You can make your relationship halal by getting a nikah (Islamic marriage) done. Most masjids can help with this, or you can contact Tayba instructors for advice.

The most important tip for a happy marriage is to put Allah and Islam first in life.

Practice the values of Islam in your marriage, such as:

The Prophet ﷺ, conveyed that the best among people are those who show the utmost kindness and compassion towards their wives and families.

KEY TO A HARMONIUS MARRIAGE

- Put effort into making the marriage work.
- Don't have too-high expectations of your spouse.
- Patience is the most important skill for a long-lasting marriage.
- Be thankful for the spouse you have and don't be negative.
- Different points of view are normal.
- Calmly express your feelings and thoughts.
- Patiently listen to those of your spouse.

The key to a happy marriage is respectful communication.

In Islam we should try not to speak to people when angry. The Prophet ﷺ said, *"If any of you becomes angry, let him keep silent"* (Ahmad). Other ways to handle anger in Islam are to say *"authu billahi minash shaytaanir rajeem"* (I seek refuge in Allah from Shaytan, the cursed) and to sit down if you are standing.

Men are responsible for providing the basic necessities and for treating their wives with kindness. The Prophet ﷺ said: *"When a Muslim spends something on his family intending to receive Allah's reward, it is regarded as charity for him"* (Sahih Bukhari). A wife's duties are to respect her husband as the leader of the family (as long as Islamic teachings are followed). Men: ensure that you can provide for a wife before considering marriage. Men and women: ensure you are ready to put another person first and to always treat them kindly and with respect.

Domestic abuse is entirely against the teachings of Islam. Ayesha (RA) said, *"The Messenger of Allah never hit a woman"* (Sahih Muslim). There are many hadiths in which the Prophet forbade men from beating their wives. If you are in an abusive relationship, seek help from your masjid and community.

- CALL -

National Domestic Violence Hotline at:

1-877-863-6338

Parenting Tips

1. Handling Guilt and Societal Expectations:

- You may feel guilt and pressure to make up for lost time with your kids. No matter what, don't parent out of guilt.
- Keep in mind that society sometimes has unrealistic expectations of parents.

2. Prioritizing Loving Connections Over Materialism:

- The best thing you can do is focus on having a loving, respectful relationship with your child.
- You cannot be too loving to your kids. Parenting is not about giving your kids lots of material things. It's about spending time with them, which shows them they are important to you.

3. Handling Bad Behavior with Empathy

- When a child does something you don't approve of, separate the child from the behavior. For instance, Say, "I feel upset about what happened," rather than "I am upset with you." Instead of labeling the child as "bad," focus on the behavior: "That was a bad choice." Remember, being open to learning from your children is important as well.

4. Prioritize Repairing the Relationship

- If you have been away from your children for a while, you may need to repair your relationship before you attempt to correct any of their behaviors. Keep in mind that children may act out at first because of how they feel about your imprisonment. Do not jump in as a disciplinarian right away. Once that relationship is repaired, then you can work on correcting behaviors, with empathy and patience.

07 Money Management:

The less you need others for money, the better off you'll be

Money management helps you avoid problems and feel more secure. First, you need to earn money. Please review Part 5: Employment on *How to Find a Job*.

Credit Union/Bank Account

It's important to open a credit union/bank account with a debit card. Here are the benefits of a bank account:

- A safe place for your money
- Putting paychecks in a bank account is cheaper than paying fees for check-cashing services
- Some employers will only put your earnings directly in your account
- A debit card means you don't have to carry lots of cash
- Online banking services allow you to keep track of your money, pay bills, and transfer money
- Apps like Venmo and Zelle let you transfer and receive money without any fees

To open a credit union/bank account, you need to bring a photo ID and at least $25-$100 to deposit. It's best to open your account at a credit union rather than at a for-profit bank. Credit unions offer the same services as banks, but because they are non-profit, they charge less fees. You can search "credit unions near me" on the internet to find a nearby credit union. When you visit the credit union, inform a worker that you want to open a checking account.

Budgeting

Budgeting means to plan your spending. You can search for "budgeting forms" online or just make your own with a notebook and pencil. Write down how much money you make in a month (income) and write down all of your expenses. Compare the two numbers and then make a plan on how much you want to spend in a month. There is a lot of information online on "how to budget."

In the beginning, you should focus on spending only on necessities and save your remaining money. Ensure that you don't spend on/commit to expenses that are greater than your income.

Credit

When you pay your bills on time, you build a good credit history and credit score. A credit score is a number that predicts how likely you are to pay back loans. Credit scores range from 350 to 800. A good credit score is any score above 670.

Having a good credit score helps you rent apartments more easily, get better car insurance rates, and more. The best way to improve your credit score is to pay bills on time and in full.

You can check your credit score online for free once a year at: annualcreditreport.com or call 1-877-322-8228

There is a difference of scholarly opinion regarding credit cards. Many Islamic scholars say that credit cards are permissible as long as you don't pay interest (i.e. you pay your entire bill on time). Debit cards are the safer option since they don't involve borrowing money.

Filing Taxes

Every year you need to file your federal and state taxes by April 15. Many people choose to file their taxes in January so they can get a tax refund sooner. To file taxes, you will need a W-2 form from your employer(s). Employers usually give you W-2 forms in January. If you are a contractor you will get a 1099 form.

You can file your taxes for free on the Internal Revenue Service (IRS) website: irs.treasury.gov/freetaxprep.

Scammers

Scamming, also called phishing, is a type of fraud in which a scammer uses a website, email, text or call to obtain your personal information. Scammers could ask for your date of birth, social security number, debit/credit card number and passwords. If you are contacted by a scammer, don't respond and don't click on any links or open any attachments.

- Be suspicious of emails or calls that offer you lots of money or "free gifts" if you pay a small fee. If the reward sounds too good to be true, avoid it.
- Scams often create a false sense of urgency. Beware of companies that try to push you into signing up for something immediately. Only sign up for services you understand. Only give personal information to companies you know to be trustworthy. Never pay for a "letter of credit."

BE AWARE

Child Support

Child support lasts until children turn 18, or 19 if they are still in high school. Managing child support payments is extremely important. If you don't pay child support, you could lose your driver's license or go to jail. If you need help with paying child support or have too little earnings, you can contact child support agencies near you.

08 Social Skills:

People and Work Skills

A famous quote says: *"Only you can do it, but you can't do it alone."* We need other people to reach our goals. Social and soft skills help us to relate to people and thus live a better life.

Communication Tips

Social skills are communication skills. Amazingly, 93% of communication is non-verbal. Only 7% of communication is verbal. People "hear" your body language and tone of voice more than your words. This is why speaking calmly is so important. Effective communication is first about active listening.

- **Here are four general communication tips:**

Speak/write clearly. If needed, speak slowly.

Choose the right time and place to communicate about heavy issues.

Decide the main purpose of your communication.

Good eye contact, posture, and body language are very important.

Islamic Manners (Adab)

Here are two hadiths that show the importance of good manners:

- "Nothing is heavier on the Scale of Deeds than one's good manners." (Sahih Bukhari)
- "The best among you in Islam are those with the best manners." (Sahih Bukhari)

And here are three hadiths about specific manners:

- "Whoever believes in Allah and the Last Day, let him speak what is good or remain silent." (Sahih Muslim)
- "Do not lose your temper." *repeated three times (Sahih Bukhari)
- "The believer does not curse/use vulgar language." (Sunan Timirdhi)

Conflict Resolution

Knowing how to disagree respectfully is the key to healthy relationships. It is a great deed in Islam to resolve conflict and make peace between people.

The Prophet ﷺ said:

"Do you know what is better than (nafl) charity, fasting and prayer? It is keeping peace and good relations between people, as quarrels and bad feelings destroy mankind." (Bukhari and Muslim)

Allah (ﷻ) says in the Quran:

"Whoever pardons and makes reconciliation, his reward is due from God." (42:40)

Tips to resolve conflict:

Remain calm; even if the other person is not.

Try to compromise. Find a solution that works for both of you.

Take a break when feeling overly emotional.

State the problem using clear language that doesn't point the finger at the other person.

Use "I-statements." An I-statement is when you begin a sentence with "I" instead of "you" so that the other person feels less threatened.
For example: *"I am upset that my coat was damaged because I can't afford to replace it."*

09 Attitudes Needed to Succeed After Release:

Success Starts from Within

"Allah does not change the conditions of a people until they change what is in themselves..." (Quran 13:11). In order to succeed, you need the right inner states.

Attitudes important for successful reentry:

REPENTANCE *(Tawbah)*

According to some, this is the most important attitude when reentering society. Tawbah means turning to Allah, seeking His forgiveness, and resolving to do what is right from now on. This attitude's motto is: "I'm going to set things right."

APPRECIATION

Appreciate everything you can: your health, food, shelter, job, family, good friends, etc. Gratitude draws more good things to you. "If you are grateful, I will certainly give you more." (Quran 14:7) If you feel that others are not appreciating you, show appreciation to yourself.

SERVICE

The Prophet ﷺ said: *"The most beloved people to Allah are those who are most beneficial to people."* Make it a habit to help others. Just making someone smile is a service to that person.

REALISM

Realism means to accept a situation as it is. Don't expect everything to happen exactly as you want. You will face obstacles–this life is a test. Realism requires that you be flexible.

HUMILITY

Humble yourself and let go of ego. Ask for help when you need it, and accept it from wherever it might come. *"He does not love the arrogant."* (Quran 16:23)

SELF-FORGIVENESS

You are not your past. When your vision is clouded by the past, it hinders your ability to see a better future. Forgive yourself and resolve to make things right. If Allah can forgive you, why not forgive yourself? *"Whoever does evil, or wrongs his soul, then seeks Allah's forgiveness, will find Allah Forgiving and Merciful."* (Quran 4:110)

RESPONSIBILITY

A common theme among people who re-offend and return to prison is: "It's always someone else's fault." Take full responsibility for your life. End the victim mentality. Acknowledge what it is you are responsible for and stop blaming others for your condition.

REMEMBRANCE (Dhikr of Allah)

Remembrance of Allah at all times will keep you on the straight path. Call on Allah and ask Him to facilitate things for you. All help is from Allah. Include Allah in your plans (e.g. marriage, jobs, etc). Remember your adab (manners) with Allah: keep up your prayers, attend Jumu'ah, and stay far away from sinful acts or environments

POSITIVITY

A positive attitude draws more positive things to you. When you notice a negative thought, replace it with a positive thought. Islam teaches us to think positively. *"If you tried to count Allah's blessings, you would never be able to number them."* (Quran 16:18) Every problem has a solution. Allah says: *"Indeed, with hardship, there is ease."* (94:5)

A good daily habit is to reflect on everything that is going right in your life. Every night before sleeping, think about what you're grateful for. Remember that being positive doesn't mean being happy all the time. It's important to acknowledge and accept all of our feelings. Being positive is about having a hopeful attitude that sees the good in every situation.

10 Self-Care:

Your Wellness Helps the World

Your emotional and physical wellness affects your worship of Allah. They affect your relationships. Caring for yourself, healing, connecting with others, and making meaning out of the past are all aspects of wellness.

Mental Health Challenges

Reentering society is not easy. Many ex-offenders experience "sensory overload"– when the five senses receive more input than they can process

Two big challenges are:

Prison life is very structured. Many ex-offenders feel overwhelmed by the lack of structure in the outside world. Performing the five daily prayers will help with this, as well as setting a daily routine of when you eat and sleep.

Your past social networks may no longer exist. You may have to create new social networks. Loneliness can tempt you to hang out with the wrong crowd. If you have mental health issues, seek treatment as soon as you're released. People who don't get treatment are more likely to return to prison.

Dealing with Trauma

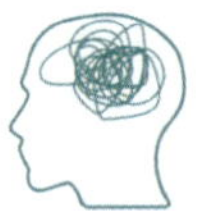

Trauma is the emotional response you have during a stressful and possibly life-changing event. Traumatic events that you had as a child can affect your adult life.

A common coping mechanism among ex-offenders is to isolate themselves, but it's better to reach out to someone. Getting professional help is a great idea. Healing from trauma involves embracing a healthier meaning of what happened.

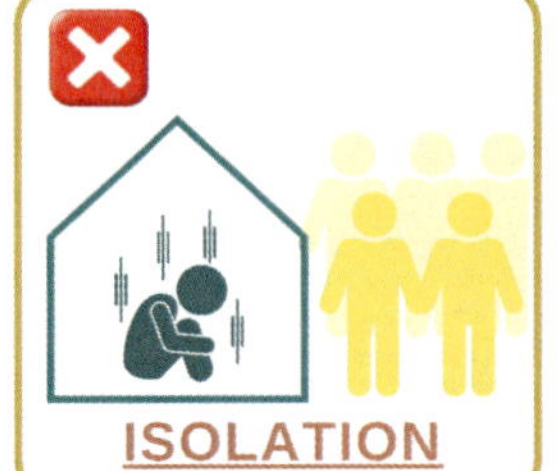

Advice on Anxiety and Depression

Anxiety & depression are the most common mental health struggles in the world.

ANXIETY

- **Anxiety** is the body's automatic fight-or-flight response and is a normal reaction to a threat.
- Anxiety isn't always bad.
- It can increase alertness and motivate you to solve problems.
- But when anxiety is overwhelming, it poses a problem.

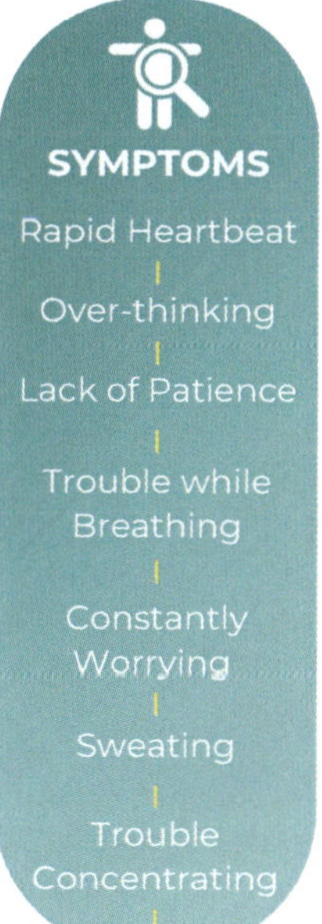

DEPRESSION

- Everyone feels down from time to time. But when feelings of hopelessness and despair won't go away, you may have **depression**.
- People describe depression as "living in a black hole."
- Men in particular may feel angry and restless.
- It's important to remember that feeling hopeless is a symptom of depression, and not reality.

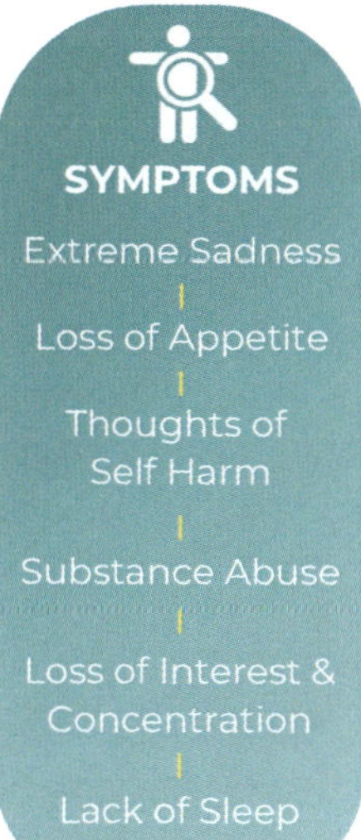

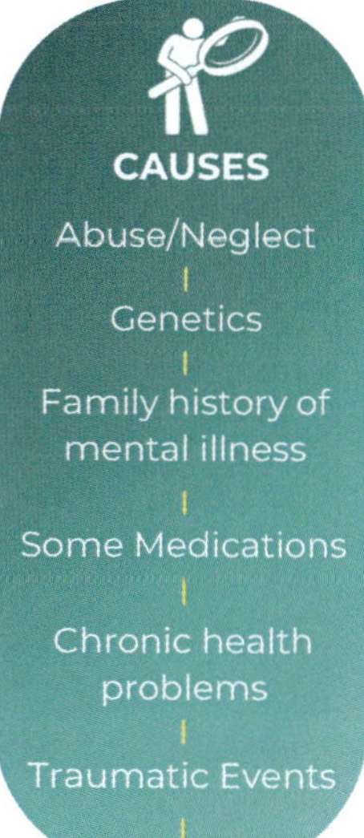

Allah says in the Quran:

> *"...Whoever fears Allah, He will make for him a way out (from every difficulty). And He will provide for him from (sources) he could never imagine." (65:2-3)*

Mental Health Resources

Below are some resources for professional mental health help. We encourage you to seek out a professional in all cases. If you prefer a Muslim, you can search for a Muslim professional. But a non-Muslim professional is (usually) better than no professional at all. Ultimately, all help is from Allah.

WE ARE HERE

TO HELP

- NAMI (National Alliance on Mental Illness) helpline: 1-800-950-6264
- National Suicide Prevention Lifeline: call 988, 1-800-273-TALK (8255) or visit 988.lifeline.org
- Search on the internet: "Muslim therapists near me".
- National Mental Health Association 1-800-969-6642
- Helpguide.org (comprehensive website about mental health topics)

Substance Abuse Advice

Reentry to society can be a time of stress, anxiety and fear. For people who have suffered from a drug problem in the past, it may return after release. Using drugs makes it harder to get a job, find housing, and have healthy relationships. Your success depends on getting help for this problem.

Ex-offenders are at greater risk of overdose. If you stopped using drugs while in prison, you will have a reduced tolerance. Your body can't handle the same amount of drugs you took before. This can lead to overdose and even death.

During stressful times it's tempting to turn to drugs. This is like putting a band-aid over a large wound.

Some tips for overcoming substance abuse:

Acknowledge it's a problem and believe that change is possible.

Step away from friends who use and get involved in negative, distracting activities.

Stay away from unnecessary prescription drugs with potential for abuse. Communicate this concern with your doctor.

Read the Tayba Foundation book Overcoming Addiction: You can request this from your Tayba instructor at any time.

Reach out to Lamps of Light, an Islamic organization focused on drug and alcohol counseling. They run a free online support group. https://www.lampsoflight.org/event

Get help through counseling or recovery programs. Call the **National Substance Abuse** Helpline: 1-800-662-HELP (4357) or search "substance abuse treatment near me" or "addiction support groups near me."

Don't let relapse keep you down. Relapse doesn't mean failure. Don't give up–learn from it. Look at what triggered the relapse, what went wrong, and what you'll do differently next time

THERE IS HOPE.
MANY PEOPLE RECOVER from SUBSTANCE ABUSE AND YOU CAN TOO, BUT YOU MUST SEEK HELP!!

Physical Health Advice

Physical wellness is taking care of your body. It's important to stay active and healthy. Exercise doesn't need to cost money; running, walking, climbing steps are all free.

Eat Healthy

Drink Plenty of Water

Get Adequate Sleep

Exercise Consistently

11 National Resources List:

There are People Who Want to Help you Succeed

Below is a list of national resources. Remember that you can search the internet/YouTube for endless information about anything.

- **211.org or call 211:** This is a free confidential service that helps people find local resources 24/7 (food, housing, healthcare, transportation, etc.)

- **Suicide Prevention Lifeline:** Call 988 or 1-800-273-TALK (8255) or visit 988.lifeline.org

- **Veterans benefits:** 1-800-393-0865 (general benefits), 1-877-424-3838 (housing benefits) or visit the website benefits.va.gov

- **Health insurance:** Visit healthcare.gov or call 1-800-318-2596.

- **Homeless services:** 1-800-569-4287 (US Department of Housing and Urban Development)

- **American Job Centers:** Job centers help you to find a job. You can search online "job centers near me" or find a center by calling the free helplines at 1-877-US-2JOBS or 1-877-889-5267.

- **Careeronestop.org:** search for jobs and find resume guides, interview tips and trainings. 1-877-872-5627.

- **National Domestic Violence Hotline:** 1-877-863-6338

- **Mental Health helpline:** 1-800-950-6264

- **Get your GED:** 1-800-626-9433.

- **Substance Abuse Help:** Call on 1-800-662-HELP (4357)

Returning to free society can be hard. As in prison, there are going to be trials and difficulties. As per the chapters in this book, you need to plan and take action to the best of your ability. Also always be mindful that these trials come from Allah, and you can overcome them with His Facilitation.

"God does not burden any soul with more than it can bear" (Qur'an 2:286).

We've included some messages of encouragement from the Tayba Foundation team below. You are in our prayers and we are here to support you on the path to success!

- Umm Ahmed, Programs Director

"Planning and implementing your reentry plan is part of your individual obligation (fard ayn) as a Muslim. Every step you take towards a successful and long-term sustained reentry is just as important as your five daily prayers, fasting, zakat, consuming halal, and every other aspect of your worship as a Muslim. Consider, with a fully dedicated heart, that your reentry plan is part of your worship as a Muslim. Maintaining your freedom, once you are released, is a daily struggle that Allah will reward you immensely for. Maintaining your freedom is also a responsibility that Allah will ask you about if you do something to lose it. There are many things that can get you sent back to prison. Avoid those like you avoid pork and alcohol. There are also many things that can help you maintain your freedom. Seek those things out and cling to them like you hold onto your religion (deen) as a Muslim."

- Shaykh Rami Nsour
Tayba Foundation Founder and Director

Don't give up! You likely dreamed of this day for so long and now you're finally here! Yes, getting re-adjusted to your new reality may be hard. You will likely face difficulties, injustices and even prejudices, but know that you will always have our support. Keep trying, keep looking forward, and focus on your personal growth and learning. This is your chance. Go get it!

- Umm Abdur - Rahman
Administrator

"And whoever is mindful of Allah, He will make a way out for them, and provide for them from sources they could never imagine. And whoever puts their trust in Allah, then He 'alone' is sufficient for them." [Quran 65:2-3]

- Sister Nusayba

Project Fatima Coach

Allah Most High says "As for those who struggle in Our cause, We will surely guide them along Our Way. And Allah is certainly with the good-doers" (Qur'an 29:69) You are engaging in a process of spiritual struggle and change. And in this matter, you are in the company of the Prophets and the foremost of the righteous. Abu Hurayra reported that the Prophet ﷺ said "Verily, an individual may have a rank with Allah that he does not achieve by good deeds. Thus, Allah continues to put him through trials with what he hates until he reaches the rank that has been destined for him." (Ibn Hibban) Due to statements like this and others from our Beloved Prophet (SAW), the scholars have said that people are tested in accordance to their rank with Allah, the Prophets being foremost in their trials. Do not consider any difficulties that you may go through as being a punishment from your Lord, but a means to shed your sins and increase your proximity to Him, as long as you are patient. Things may get hard, but remember that Allah tests those whom He loves and our ultimate happiness lies in our reliance and contentment with Him. And if you are ever feeling overwhelmed and need someone to talk to, we are but a phone call away.

- Lumumba K. Shakur

Instructor

Made in the USA
Middletown, DE
12 November 2024

64309979R00024